Gathering the pieces of days

A year in poetry

LeeAnn Pickrell

For information contact:
Unsolicited Press
Portland, Oregon
www.unsolicitedpress.com
orders@unsolicitedpress.com
619-354-8005

Book Design: Kathryn Gerhardt
Editor: Kristen Marckmann
ISBN: 978-1-963115-38-3

To Josh, a piece of each day

Contents

Preface   7

January   9

February   15

March   21

April   29

May   35

June   43

July   49

August   55

September   63

October   69

November   77

December   83

Preface

On the first day of 2018 I set myself the task of writing a page each morning about the day previous. At the end of a week—beginning with Monday and ending with Sunday—I would take those seven days and create a page or so of what struck me about that week. In 2019 I took those fifty-two weeks and wrote a poem for each week of 2018. It took me a year to complete them and several months of revisions and then the COVID-19 pandemic swept the world and we shut down. Gone suddenly were the coffees with friends, trips to the Oakland Symphony, Oakland A's baseball games, long dinners with friends, concerts, traveling, gatherings we held every year, chance encounters. We no longer said hello with pecks on the cheek or hugs or even handshakes, maybe an elbow bump, but mostly we stepped away from each other—at least six feet—and waved. We canceled vacations, family get-togethers, weddings. We covered our faces with masks. And I started to wonder if any of these poems of ordinary life mattered. At moments it seemed we would never go back to the way it was, or if we even should; certainly many things needed to change. And now that our lives are crowded again with deadlines and obligations, family and friends, calendars whose days are full, I find myself forgetting that for one year I paid close enough attention to capture these moments. If I learned anything from the pandemic, it's this—how precious the pieces of each day are and how easily and unexpectedly they can be scattered and lost.

October 2024

January

–1–

Drove a loop
hugging the coast on a ribbon of gray

Moleskine months laid out in a grid,
spreads of weeks to make a year

Black rocks from a pond, raked
to surround cement stepping stones

Coffee to keep working, giving up to nap,
dreaming of jelly donuts and Elizabeth I

Tree to untrim, blue and silver balls, lights unstrung and coiled,
ornaments wrapped and stored

Ikea list: stool for Henry the cat, Swedish meatballs,
Lördagsgodis—Swedish pick-and-mix

Josh's morning confession of accidently mixing in
decaf with the regular all week

I gather the pieces of days
of waking and the sun's rise
hidden by the night's storm,
drops and plops of rain on the roof,
a grumpy, soggy day of stomping in rain puddles.
I meet a friend for an afternoon latte,
and still the white strands of Christmas lights
weep from the trees' branches
like twinges of self-pity I call sad.
Dinner is a stew of January's leftovers.
Afterward, at a friend's open house, a man asks:
What inspires your poetry?

–3–

Mantras of morning—
coffee more coffee
pages to write
lunches to make,
of workdays and editing Jung—
"Lost Voices of the Feminine"
"Beyond Narcissism" …
"The Birth of the Self."

Litanies of what I did and didn't do
what I could or should have done,
four hours lost driving in the rain
to South City and back.
The lie I tell on a trail
in Leona Heights Park,
a canyon of boulders and fallen trees:
A man asks, "How was
the women's march this morning?"
And I, pointing to my pink pussy hat, say,
"Oh, this was from last year's march,"
as if I had been there.

Chants of evening
as a friend lies on the floor of the vet's exam room
with Reggie, a pit bull fought as a pup

so anxious now he eats his paws.
Tears on every face, the vet's, the tech's, mine,
while my friend cries and chants the Hare Krishna
the vet listening for a heartbeat until it's gone.

Songs of night,
at the Oakland Symphony,
wearing the purple and black scarf
I bought at the Galeries Lafayette in Paris
when I was twenty-five, held together
with my mother's black rose pin,
swaying the symphony's version of
"Swing Low, Sweet Chariot."

–4–

A week of flavors like jazz
piquant peppers
jalapeños and pickled scallions
mussels in a butter wine sauce

At the Warriors game, Golden State nachos
with chicken and cheese, guac, sour cream
and sprinkled bacon bits while players dribble
shoot three pointers from downtown
make slam dunks and alley-oops

At the museum's white elephant sale
bypassing ice skates and scuba gear
full sets of dead relatives' china
dolls dressed in boxes, feather boas and furs,
for chihuahua salt and pepper shakers
and a red-chili-pepper-shaped salsa bowl
with a green spoon for a stem

February

–1–

An article I edit claims that when we sleep our soul
lifts out of our body to cavort with spiritual beings.
Between awake and asleep tea and a coconut tart.
My cousin comes for dinner, telling family stories of my uncle,
his dad, who just died at almost ninety.
I miss the blood-red blue moon,
catch only a slice of white beyond the edge of earth's shadow
Watch Henry the cat for signs of breath,
laying my head on his bed not ready to let him go,
knowing it shouldn't be my grief that decides.
I dress in black for brunch with a friend from Montana,
spend a day writing two poems and to end the week
C tosses the key from her balcony at the corner of Hyde and
        Green.
Poets talking poetry and loneliness and counting our steps
each day as if it matters being minor poets.
I wake on almost Monday to Henry sick in the night,
carrying him back to bed, where we lie together,
my hand light on his back
until I fall asleep again.

–2–

Saturday afternoon and
I hike the Belgium Trail
to the site of a sanitarium

where the wealthy once sent
their insane, alcoholic, and drug addled

The park sign describes Friday night dances
where cows now graze among palm trees
and the remains of a crumbled foundation hidden in grass

where I sit among them holding
three deaths in two weeks in my hand

the uncle who loved farming
and building mechanical things
Mimi the godmother of bangles and beads

And Henry the cat who kept me here
awake on this earth

who let me hold him as we drove
down the hill to the vet,
looking around at the view

then back at me—quiet and still

–3–

sparklers on the back deck
year of the dog I christen cat

wake late to work dreams
sentences that left for the beach
formatting nightmares

Ethiopian coffee in bed
single origin sex
iced coffee to wake again

Brahm's First Symphony
driving through fields of green and brown
continuous rain and windshield wipers
rushing to keep up
with base and bassoon
clarinet and oboe
a timpani of thunder and lightning
as we walk past the lighthouse at Asilomar
violins tiptoeing between tidepools
where black and red crabs
as small as my pinky finger
pick their way over rocks and empty shells
the crescendo back home as I slam
my palms down on the desk
Now I know why you get scared when I get angry
and in the quiet that follows
when everyone has left and the day empties
I hear Henry in the next room
jump off the bed and skitter
a toy mouse across the floor
spirit cat

March

I follow a river of brown
coffee spilled from a cup full to the brim
falling from my hands
spattering pillows
running along the wall behind the bed
where I find a week's detritus gathered.
Grumpy and dressed in black,
piano concertos on headphones as I work—
Chopin who died of consumption,
the literary disease,
what E joked she had
when she called from Nicaragua
to say she had been coughing up blood;
another day's office wear of
pink-and-black polka dot pajamas;
more coffee at Cole's
a café table for two and across the street
cyclists and bikers in spandex and leather;
browsing the used bookstore for Nordic crime novels;
migrating from bed to sofa on a sleepless night
waking to rain tap-dancing on the rooftop.

Macro instructions:

CTRL-Emails
    declare themselves
    NOW NOW NOW
    Queen Homonym at work
    rain-reign-rein

CTRL-SHIFT-Purple
    robe I wear to work
    color of royalty
    from the purple prickly pear
    discovered in an old new world

ALT-Pause
    to breathe
    dance to my own songs
    a futile search through cabinets for chocolate

ALT-Yoga
    chai and a
    twenty-minute savasana
    bolsters blankets pillows for my eyes

CTRL-ALT-Museum
>of postcard poems
>in boxes glued to the wall
>ready to mail
>stamped with the poet's likeness

ALT-Coffee
>and Costco
>a mile up and down aisles
>sloshing through purposeful puddles of rain

ALT-SHIFT-Spring
>forward
>the foretelling

Catching up with my mom
on a Sunday hard to remember
after days of rain.
A dead car and an Uber
whose driver insists on asking questions.
Letting calls go that would be easier to answer
than trying to explain myself by text.
Boxes I'm going through only to store away again:
journals of scribbled angst
pictures in broken frames.

But then I go into the kitchen to cook
to mark the turn of day to evening
and passing across the back deck
a brown-striped tabby with a green collar
—a neighbor's cat, I tell myself—
but gone so fast I know it's Henry
passing through seams of time and space.

The wonder of rain and more rain
mud and puddles
lobster ravioli with shrimp and avocado
clouds parting to blue sky
Mexican mochas

At the symphony Rossini and Schubert
overtures and preludes
Soul Restoration, a tribute to Oakland:
Lake Merritt and Eastmont Mall,
Huey Newton and the Black Panthers
East 14th and International Blvd.
MC Hammer and Run-D.M.C.

Sunday afternoon and the first game of the season
an exhibition game between the A's and the Giants
We're robbed of a homerun and outplayed
but we have a clear sightline to home plate
and the sun warms our backs
and it's spring again

The week before Easter I sort the days into lines

On Monday I dream I've been awake for sixteen years
    two-and-a-half spent reading the news

On Tuesday I don't dye Easter eggs
    pink, lavender, green, yellow, blue

On Wednesday I'm pulled in six directions
    east, west, north, south, up, down

On Thursday I scream coffee, more coffee!
    and the altar is draped in black

On Friday I wear black
    shirt, pants, shoes

On Saturday I trip on stepping stones
    the A's rally but not enough to win

On Sunday I don't take a photo before church
    me in my new Easter dress, hat, white patent-leather shoes
    I don't go to church; I eat a scone with lemon curd

April

–1–

Editing a book on sandplay, therapy
to bring the unconscious to consciousness.
I think beach sand finding its way into dark corners.
Drinking three cups of coffee, perpetual work and rain.
Talking to a woman who can't stop drinking.
Playing the sixties, Danish jazz meets the Flintstones,
a dark club, a sunny Sunday.

Dim Sum in San Diego
char siu bao, shumai, no chicken feet
depth charges and
banana chocolate-chip pancakes
a sampling of olive oils
mango lassi and heart burn

Freshly roasted peanuts
at the Giants game in San Francisco
with Ghirardelli hot chocolate
and a Pablo Sandoval foul ball
—my first foul ball!—
in the bottom of the eighth
raising my arm above my head
victorious

We find ourselves in darkness, not light.
Water falls from the fountain in the café's garden
and the stones start sliding down.

A friend has decided to live as a blind person who can see
rather than a sighted person who can't.
Not in light but in darkness we find ourselves.

Three runs in the bottom of the first and the A's are winning.
Top of the sixth, bases loaded, and a first pitch grand slam,
and the game starts falling apart.

We attend a play about Vietnamese refugees
at a camp in Arkansas, exposing a generational divide.
In darkness, not light, we find ourselves.

The father to his son: when you say the Americans were wrong
you discount my sacrifice, the sacrifices of the South Vietnamese,
and our words start rearranging themselves.

New kitties and everything is upside-down.
Escaping behind the bed's drawers, they're lost
in the dark, we need the light to find them.
Taking the bed apart, the slats start slipping out.

Who will read these poems
of ordinary life?
Of days I can hardly remember.
Of overreactions when a client asks:
did you send the index to layout?
and I explode, "Fuck this!"
pound my fists on the desk.
Of Josh saying, "That's really not
an appropriate way to act."
Of walks through tall grass and
wildflowers—more poetic.
Of raising my hands overhead
"Hello World! Good Morning!"
Of seared flat iron steaks
bread pudding with mushrooms
pappardelle with spicy pork ragu.
Of conversation light and animated.
Of a rift that leads to a night together
but separate, doing our own things.
Of going through photos and seeing
in my face my mother's face exact.
Of trees and rooflines and a deep
blue-green bay.
Of earth and its curves.

May

1

Doing the hustle of work and coffee, then switching to pop and singing along with my Adele station that doesn't play Adele but songs by songwriters like Adele. Doing the cha-cha with the piles on my desk. The kitties waltzing with sunbeams. The hills in the dog park where we walk are alive with lupine and wild cucumber. At a performance in San Francisco—*Unbound, Snowblind, Anima Animus*—the ballet of my finger as it circles the cup's lid, searching for the opening in the dark, bringing the coffee to my mouth to drink, sensing my mother in every movement I make. Cinco de Mayo and a pitcher's duel through the bottom of the 9th inning, a flamenco of cutters and sliders and fastballs, two-seam and four, making it home in time to see Kris Davis walk it off with a show-tune homerun in the bottom of the 12th.

Connections	Disconnections
Pookie doesn't want to stand up	I panic—the cat is sick
just wants his belly rubbed	Josh's back goes out
halfway across the street	tempted by pain meds
when I was twenty-one	my boyfriend broke a foot
didn't settle for coffee, a talk	we both took his Vicodin
up up up the hill	K makes a scratching post
I order a scratching post	from discarded carpet
delivered to the door in a box	the A's score first
we split a Georgia peach Italian ice	but lose to the Astros
with vanilla frozen custard	a sinking sadness
saying I'll walk first thing	in the morning but don't
sending flowers for Mother's Day	call to leave a message
she calls back to say she's been lonely	knowing I should do more

–3–

Monday's marine layer dissipates
and the sky reveals itself
as I rake the meditation garden
water the flowering cherry, Japanese maple,
our first trees just planted.

The routine of a day whose edges are crisp:
coffee, two cups at least,
a page of words, connected or not.

Do I confess to praying
to remembering the quiet
amid the cacophony of thoughts, ideas, grievances?

The cats take their first trip to the vet
and I look down to discover
I'm still wearing slippers.

I overhear a woman going on about her book editor
for her soon-to-be-published book.

I think first: I hate her.
I think second: well, she might have an editor
but I am an editor.

We go to the symphony on Friday night—
Bernstein's *Serenade,* for Violin and Orchestra,
inspired by *Plato's Symposium,* five philosophers
expounding on love,
Tchaikovsky's sixth symphony.

The conductor speaks of him dying
nine days after the premiere
from cholera or arsenic.

I watch a royal wedding of dresses and fascinators
that I swear I will never admit to watching.

I wake up dreaming of waking up
to discover I'm still asleep.

out for a burger with a friend
think of getting one for Josh but don't

feeling his feeling put upon
that I take take take

lying down with cats   lights out
falling toward sleep

CRASH from the next room
the vase of roses rolling across the floor

a waterfall streaming down from the table
cats scattering then gathering again

rain clears the decks
like that first sip of coffee in bed

alone in the house editing
fitting work in between the cracks

dancing "on point" in the living room
in my pink "Hello Gorgeous" pajamas

possessed by the gods the A's
homer three times off three first pitches

and Mengden pitches a complete game shutout
celebrate with mint chip and orange chocolate

in a sugar cone at iScream in Berkeley
not ever waking all the way on a sleepy Sunday

5

Hump day, dump day, make the bed, start over.
A day I say the thing I shouldn't say.
I nag, he explodes, and we do our dance:
Just drop me at BART, I say. I won't be
going wherever it is we're going, but I do.
We break up an afternoon of errands
with lime popsicles dripping down our arms.
I write a ghazal about Texas in a
May sonnet on a drive out to Seal Rock
on the first day that feels like summertime.
In the Zen Garden, raking grooves in the rocks—
  a rake of hickory marking the swirls
   of a week around the flax and maple tree.

June

–1–

Strings of memory
I follow through the week:
Vermeer's *The Music Lesson*
on the page of a calendar
and I'm on the piano bench,
the teacher with her strict red
bouffant hair sitting behind me,
"You'll never learn if you don't practice."
Fourteen years later at twenty-two,
still undisciplined about certain things—
waking after hardly any sleep
so my parents can drive me to
the treatment center; for weeks
I wonder why I didn't drink all night
if I had known it would be the last time.
Thirty-two years ago this week.
Driving down the Arlington lost in thought
hugging the road's curves
I swerve to miss the car
half off the road back to today.

–2–

Flying to Ohio,
  the plane descending
  over gray Lake Erie
for five days in Oberlin

  a slowing down
as I sleep under the attic eaves
of a house three stories tall

That first morning
  a cardinal perched
    in the tree outside
    the kitchen window
  a trip to the farmer's market
  where I'm serenaded

Midsummer's eve approaches
  and still twilight at nine
    an evening walk down Elm
    and up Professor Street
  Then bursts of light
    —fireflies!—
everywhere flickering
luminescence
    above thick green lawns

—3—

What I did on my summer vacation

A Pilgrimage to Akron and a preserved house
where Dr. Bob lived and Bill the stockbroker stayed.
The kitchen still set up for coffee and morning meditation.
The son's room where the drunks sobered up,
"prescribed" sauerkraut, tomato juice, and Karo syrup.

Cleveland is pastrami on rye,
pickled carrots in Ohio City,
last stop on the Underground Railroad,
the church where lookouts climbed
the steeple to watch for the boats
crossing Lake Erie from Canada.
The Rock & Roll Hall of Fame—
Elvis and the Beatles, Motown and Detroit,
CBGBs and New York,
the Sex Pistols and Ramones,
years of *American Bandstand* clips,
the Cars and Tom Petty and
"My Guitar Gently Weeps."
Baseball after a two-hour rain delay.

A slice of Pittsburgh in twenty-four hours—
doormen in suits greet us at the haunted Omni William Penn,

crossing Roberto Clemente Bridge over the Allegheny River,
its fence filled with love locks, to a ballgame at Three Rivers
        Stadium,
more rain, breakfast at Dor-Stop, driving past neighborhoods of
brick houses, everyone telling us to ride the Duquesne Incline
to see Pittsburgh's three rivers but we never did.

–4–

Little lies I tell: Josh can't remember whether he bought the tickets
to the Giants' game or I did—I claim I got them for his birthday;

or saying I heard him when I really only heard fragments of words.
His two nights of migraines, trip to the ER, home in time

to brew coffee for the next morning. The cat Pookie hopping
around with an elephant-shaped cone on his head after

worrying a spot on his leg raw. Meeting K at Dosa by Dosa for
dinner. Yoshi's Jazz Club on Friday for Josh's 59th:

an Oakland A's sushi roll with avocado, tempura shrimp,
cod, blood orange sorbet and jazz for dessert.

A jacuzzi morning, a delicious Saturday afternoon nap.
Running into a neighbor's sister at Zachary's pizza.

She remembers Josh's kindness when her brother
was dying. Smoke and ash fill the air from fires north

and east. An op-ed in *The New York Times* says resistance
is listening to music, playing it, reading a book, writing a poem.

July

–1–

A Monday email
    Thanks for pulling it together.

Fireworks over the Bay on Tuesday
    symphonic sounds
        patriotic tunes and
            a *Mamma Mia* sing-along

A dream perchance of Wednesday's
    Independence Day Sale at Nordstrom's
        Josh says I've become demanding
            He just wants me to be happy

Still the Thursday morning
    not much work, a nap, and later
        Shrimp Diablo with jalapeños
            tomatoes and golden raisins

Gray quiet Friday
    train's horn sounding in the distance
        La Bamba tacos and watching the movie *It*
            a shape shifter who becomes my fears

Wake on Saturday recalling a trip to Milwaukee   a wedding
      on the shore of a great lake forty years ago and the friend
           who lay in my bed in Dallas recovering from the
                abortion she couldn't tell her mom about

A Sunday that begins as Sunday
      and ends with notes to an author
           about periods and ellipses

A half caf rather than full
this won't keep me awake
and the thought I ponder
whether perhaps it's time
to let go of my childhood
sitting on the roof of the garage
fogged in and freezing
listening to virtuosos jamming
on their violins and drums
eating toast with Irish Gold butter
here on the walkway

still I can't sleep
a dream of black hair
sprouting from my chest
that I'm desperate to pluck
but can't at a party where
I know Josh and the host
and the thought that this
would be more fun drunk
laughter and peaches
Josh asks me to dance
there in front of the house

Lost and found days
Watching fireworks with an 80s soundtrack
from the third deck of the Oakland Coliseum
Getting a deep red, almost purple mani-pedi
Putting one foot in front of the other periodically sinking
Finally feeling better after that second nap with the cat
Asking myself: How much coffee can I drink?
Surprised how much it hurts to burn my hand
       on the poblano pepper oil
A five-year-old asks: Why do you have your pajamas on again?
The As walk off in the bottom of the 11th on a single by Lucroy
Walking to Poinsettia Park
where my friend's son feeds us omelets from the play stove
bacon sticks from the playground
A week of mud pie days
All those mud pies I used to dump in the pool, get in trouble for

Paraprosdokian
the latter part of a
sentence or phrase
or this poem perhaps
of a day in which
the end turns the
beginning on its head
Sleeping in and sipping
slow cups of coffee into
afternoon to cap a weekend
restful and free in a house
of language pivots
Night falls and I
switch positions
side, front, back, side
some shift that will
turn off mind
allow sleep to enter
waking to see Josh
sitting on the bedside
like it's morning
so disappointedly tired
until he turns off
the light for bed

August

–1–

A July
I've been
calling June
comes to
an end

    Maple leaves dry brown
    crackling around their edges
    hot winds from the east

Home is the books I carry from one dwelling to the next: the five-pound Shakespeare from college, Poe's *Complete Works* found in a used bookstore in Dallas, all those Greek tragedies. The journals filled and stored, now in the garage, from second grade—J kissed me—to next time I won't have more than three drinks, as if writing it could make it happen, to years of resentments and fears and "why me?" The few pieces published. Framed photos of my grandmother in her 1918 hairbow and my father in his WWII naval aviator gear. An antique desk from my grandparents into which I carved my name in fifth grade.

Caprese salad
heirlooms burrata basil
taste of summertime

–2–

Two dreams and a photograph

A room redone
       splitting apart
glass walls looking into yards
where children play
I want to talk about the time
we went out twenty-seven years ago
          unclear who the other half of we is
searching for my car
in a city more like Cleveland Heights

Coming across a photo taken in Chico:
I'm fortyish leaning against my
electric blue Mini Cooper
wearing faded jeans and a navy t-shirt
with the name of a local band
an inch of still smooth tan skin
between the jeans and my shirt

Slipping the edges
all that's left in a performance of sorts
a theater in a vast cavernous space

stage far below
viewed from seats above
exposed walls and beams

–3–

For a day
the A's have tied
the Astros for
first place;
the next day
it's back to second
place—these
are the images
I sort into files,
along with high fives,
pitches elevated
over the plate,
sitting with Josh's
brother in the
salmon-colored
courtyard,
shuffling in and out,
a country I know
only from dreams,
making my mother
laugh when I tell her
I also use subtitles
to watch TV
especially for
those British mysteries.

I picture her
moving slowly
about her apartment
in Dallas
when she says
at eighty-seven
she feels more
fragile now.

—4—

All I had to do
was cancel
reschedule ahead
saying I forgot
for not picking up
when I don't get my way
I'll call right back
as soon as I finish
this or that
knowing I won't
pretending to listen
never heard
saying sure, yeah
past blackberry brambles
and grass

lying to a friend
I was just about to call
the instant she called me
my propensity
for whining
errors I should have caught
"pubic" for "public"
leaving out the author's
acknowledgments
saying I never got it
when I knew I had
in the car or on our walk
to whatever was asked
so I miss the sky
Josh beside me

–5–

Two games
in a homestand
against the Mariners:
the first
with a tailgate—
shrimp ceviche tostadas
and fruit salad
with melon balls.
The A's come back
to make it a one-run
game in the bottom
of the eighth,
not enough to walk off
but fireworks afterwards
exploding over
the coliseum's
upper deck.

The second game
watched on TV.
Josh in the living room;
I'm in the bedroom.
We yell back and forth
between pitches and runs
as the A's thrash the Mariners,
8 to 2 we celebrate.

September

A laborless day of sleeping, napping, a walk to get out of, watching *Bull Durham,* about the hot-shot young pitcher and the catcher who's been in the minors for twelve years with a twenty-day call-up to The Show. The absence of contact between us, gaps that can grow into crevasses we can cross with laughter, announcing to "CNN" all the good things we've done to assuage the other's disappointment: trash dispersed into bins, dishes dispensed to cabinets. Look what I did! What I did! Then at the nail salon, as our toes dry green with yellow *A*s to celebrate an A's potential playoff run, a bride and her bridesmaids are getting their nails done. We offer advice to the bride, as if we know: have a sense of humor; after you fight, laugh; you won't always like each other, but it will pass; hire someone to clean; dance anyway. At the end of *Bull Durham,* the catcher's been cut again, facing the end of a career that never became what he wanted, but he's dancing in the candlelit living room with Annie who teaches players the religion of baseball. A hot night moves toward fall and the end of the season.

–2–

My niece turns twenty-one
three days after I turn fifty-five.
In the photo my sister-in-law sends
from my niece's dinner with her boyfriend,
in the photo Josh takes at lunch,
our desserts focus the frame,
with a glass of champagne for my niece,
a cappuccino in the foreground for me.
A toast to the photographers
and a plum galette with
the candle burning above
cardamom ice cream, crushed
pistachios, and bittersweet chocolate
drizzled over cake and a coconut gelato.

–3–

On the first day I consider writing a novel with an alcoholic
detective who doesn't get drunk each time something bad happens.

On the second I review all the cities I've visited on my weather
app: Pacific Grove, San Diego, Oberlin, Cleveland, Pittsburgh.

The third I ask as we sign our trusts with advanced directives
if I get Alzheimer's like my dad and his mom, can I be put down?

The fourth day I dream of the State Fair of Texas, walking through
a forest of campers, leaving my flip flops on the gondola.

The fifth we almost leave when Trevino gives up the lead, then
Canha steps to the plate with a two-run shot into the bleachers.

The sixth day equals the night and a yoga teacher
tells me to write the story of my pelvis.

On the seventh day a slow game and a drunken Trump supporter
who claims we can agree to disagree because we both love the A's.

The first full week of autumn and Big Tex welcomes us to the State Fair of Texas with "Howdy Folks" and Fletcher's corny dogs. After the pig races and arroz con leche—fried rice balls with Blue Bell vanilla ice cream, we sit with a Black couple from Houston, where my mother taught at the same school the man later attended. They talk education and hurricanes, developers developing in flood zones where poor people live, his work as a minister, hers as a teacher, segregation and integration, court-ordered busing in the 1970s, more than twenty years after *Brown.* My mom tells him how she ran for the school board and lost, that she was on the Urban League, appointed to the Tri-Ethnic committee by the judge who ordered busing in Dallas.

> The man tells her, "You're a hero."
> Then turning toward me, he says, "Your mom is a hero."

She responds before I can. "Oh, she was always irritated with me then." I was thirteen, in middle school; it was 1976, and I didn't understand what she was risking. She says, "My husband used to say, 'Mary Ann, if you don't stop, we're going to wake up to crosses burning on our lawn.'"

> I decide: I'm going to tell her
> I think she's a hero too.
> Before I leave to fly back home to Oakland
> into the unexpected fog of late September.
> But I don't.

October

–1–

The week begins
with the first rain
and ends dry and hot
with Diablo winds
in between sentences that
spill one into the next
as the sun rises later
over the hill and the
nights of fall lengthen
and the A's lose to the
Yankees in the wild card
game and like that
the season is over.

We've entered the eucalyptus days of fall.
My mother writes casually about stumbles
over the last week—"bought a walker."
The symphony opens with three dance episodes
from Bernstein's *On the Town,* followed by
Rachmaninoff's second piano concerto
and Shostakovich's fifth symphony—
an apology to Stalin, the conductor says, but not really.
A trip to Cloverdale to see kiln-fired ceramic whales,
inhaling the crush of October grapes,
getting lost following the Gravenstein Highway home.

–3–

Eleven people—
mothers, fathers,
sons, daughters—
massacred at a
synagogue in Pittsburgh.

A naming service to celebrate new life.

Rearranging the living room,
rearranging lives that shouldn't
need rearranging.

I drift in a dense,
fogged-in forest
at the edge of a bog,
the start of a dream,
before my eyes open
and I'm back in my seat
at the concert of Danish jazz.

On our walk the sounds
of children cut the morning's silence.

–4–

Circles and loops
etched grooves

unintentional weeding of a day

First question of the week:
        What would I do for my next act?

            A barista in a bookstore café
            An usher at Oakland A's games

Orange polish on our toes
a black spider spinning its web

Coffee, slippers,
pad to kitchen to slice apples
top off coffee again

So many days
full of potential

Some days I don't get dressed

Second question of the week:
        A nap or coffee or both?

Both

Melatonin dream
I work for the Queen of England
can't leave until she does

Consider the week in all its colors

Making a list of all the places
I've lived—Greenwillow, Forest Bend,

the dorm at Arizona State, that
apartment in Denton, off Greenville Ave.

in Dallas—does treatment count or the
halfway house? …, seventeen addresses

if you don't include all the times
back and forth to my parents.

Letting the day drag forward on Norma's deck
as she reads to me from her book of life.

Cat in my lap in the chair by the front
window, waiting for trick or treaters who

never come. Day of the Dead sugar skulls
recalling those graveyard visits to the Pickrell Plot

in Phoenix—filled now—where the family
picnicked during reunions. In savasana

considering how often I've lost touch
or never followed up, or what really happened

hard to pin down now. Time turning back again,
pink and orange sunset as October falls.

November

1

Gray ash from fires
coating the deck   To the south
Santa Anas whip the embers
toward Malibu and Thousand Oaks
where a gunman killed 12 dancers
a week ago, a country-western bar
college night   In the north
Diablo winds fan the flames
Paradise is burning

at a friend's fiftieth
she brings the shelves
of her life together
a band plays 80s hits
Josh and I slip outside
to dance in front of the
window a friend watches
as we swing wide and spin
coming together again

–2–

A week that goes

    from Yoshi's jazz
        and sushi and
            pretending I didn't
                see my ex-husband

    to a 100-degree fever
        at daybreak, drinking
            Josh's special chai and
                napping into afternoon

    to Josh's job shut down
        the inspector's citation for
            an unpermitted dwelling, the
                ground shifting under our feet

    to a *Requiem for Ghost Ship*
        for cello and orchestra
            escapes blocked and a staircase
                of pallets crashing down

to the Camp Fire still
        burning after a week
                each day getting worse
                        Paradise destroyed

–3–

The eve of Thanksgiving
and my mother texts
from Baton Rouge that
Will's showing pictures
from their trip to Europe,
just like our grandfather
used to do, sitting us down
for hours in their living room
in Prescott, the slides in
black and white
projected on the screen.
This year it's just the two
of us and steaks for dinner.
Twenty years or more
since my brothers and I
have gathered for a holiday
I miss for a moment,
yet the rain has cleared
the smoke from the fires north,
95 percent containment now,
and the next day we
sit out drinking coffee
in the early morning, reading
that turns into talking and a
fresh morning bun.

–4–

The week ends with a drive down 280 to a holiday party in Woodside and almost missing my exit while listening to Casey Kasem's Top 40 from the early 80s, Kenny Rogers and "Lady" topping the pop charts at #1, and memories of my first trip to San Francisco when I was in sixth grade, wearing yellow toe socks and a blue skirt, riding down this same road to Palo Alto and how green and rolling the hills were; the same trip where a mime got married on a cable car and the conductor played the wedding march, and I announced, "I'm going to move here someday," which I did, and get married on a cable car, which I didn't; the same trip where we went wine tasting in Napa and after my first glass of wine, which my parents had gotten for me, I went back for a second and the waiter said loudly as I reached for the glass, "And you're twenty-one?" which I wasn't, being twelve, and I slunk back to my parents who whispered, "We'll get you another glass."

December

–1–

A walk around and up,
the rug pulled out
to reveal a not-there floor,
memories that aren't mine—
a photograph of my parents
on their wedding day, December 5,
fifty-six years ago, my mother
in a navy wool suit and matching
pillbox hat, a black rose pin
on her lapel that I wear now.
My father in a dark brown suit,
his thick eyebrows framing
his open face. We're a family
that does better the second time,
second marriages, second
chances when the shine is
scuffed, when I can meet
a friend for coffee and discover
I left the house still wearing
my slippers and it's not
the end of everything.

2

Christmas Tree Lane in Alameda
and a dream of crossing
a block of houses ringed by
the Trinity River to Oak Cliff,
lights, cardboard Santas
raging and wild, a tram
of elves and their workshop,
the sleigh pulled by reindeer
there and back and a nightclub with
a mechanical Abominable Snowman
that's a pool that's a room
with a toothache, the land of misfit
toys. Our own tree trimmed
but bare underneath. Twelve hours
of footnotes and presents wrapped
in green and gold to the strains of
Nina Simone and Fats Domino.

–3–

On kitchen counters
evidence of the cats'
secret night journeys

Christmas trees painted
on our toes   green glitter
dabs of colored balls

My dad would have been
97 today   His last question
when I said I loved him, Really?

In the dog park a tree decorated
with random ornaments of rainbow
clouds, Santa heads, a silver star on top

–4–

Last week of the year
waking to "Santa Baby …
come on down the chimney to me,"
singing Christmas carols, sharing
a songbook with my mom, stealing
secret Santa gifts and winding up
with Shakespearian Insult band-aids.
Eating biscuits and gravy for brunch
and shrimp tacos for dinner with two
of my oldest friends on the same day.
Telling my mother what I've always
wanted to say: she's a hero to me.
Seeing her off at the airport, trying
to keep her tears from falling with
promises *to see you soon,* undressing
the tree, storing the ornaments away
until next Christmas, a dream of making
pizza pies for a retreat in India
without the ingredients, which I used
for something else, then wanting to die
like those dreams of drinking
then waking relieved I'm still sober,
waking relieved I want to live,
discovering windows where there
had been walls during this
last week of the year.

Acknowledgments

I want to thank the editors of the following journals in which some of these poems first appeared:

February, week 4, appeared as "Rain Symphony" in *Loud CoffeePress.*

March, weeks 1–5, appeared in the *Atlanta Review.*

October, week 1, appeared as "The Week Begins" in *Spitball.*

February, week 3, appeared as "February"; June, week 4, as "Resistance"; and December, week 1, as "Seconds" in *MacQueen's Quinterly.*

August, week 1, October week 3, October, week 4, appeared in *Red Wolf Leaflets* and *Wondrous Leaflets.* September, week 1, appeared in *Wondrous Leaflets.*

November, week 4, appeared as part of a two-part poem titled "Communion" in *Unbroken.*

In March –4– : *Soul Restoration* was created by Oakland artist Kev Choice.

In November –2– *Requiem for Ghost Ship*, a concert presented by the Oakland Symphony, commemorated those lost in the December 2016 Ghost Ship fire in Oakland, California.

Thanks to Clare MacQueen, founding editor of *MacQueen's Quinterly,* who has created a space for so many poets and their poems. Knowing an editor truly appreciates your work, whether accepted or not, is a great gift.

I also want to thank my Sunday poetry group, for they are part of all these poems.

This book contains so many pieces of my extraordinary ordinary life, and I am so grateful to all you who have been with me on this journey. You are in the words of these poems. Specifically I want to thank my mother, Mary Ann Pickrell, and Josh Rubenstein, my partner and always my first and last reader.

About the Author

LeeAnn Pickrell is a poet, editor, and managing editor of *Jung Journal: Culture & Psyche*. Her work has appeared in a variety of online and print journals, including *One Art, MacQueen's Quinterly, Loud Coffee Press, Atlanta Review, West Marin Review, Eclectica, where* she was a Spotlight Poet, and the anthologies *Coffee Poems* and *A Gathering of Finches*. Her chapbook *Punctuated* was published in 2024 by Bottlecap Press, and her book *Tsunami* is forthcoming in 2026, also from Unsolicited Press. She lives in Richmond, California, with her partner and two fabulous cats, and has an MFA from Mills College.

About the Press

Unsolicited Press is based out of Portland, Oregon and focuses on the works of the unsung and underrepresented. As a womxn-owned, all-volunteer small publisher that doesn't worry about profits as much as championing exceptional literature, we have the privilege of partnering with authors skirting the fringes of the lit world. We've worked with emerging and award-winning authors such as Amy Shimshon-Santo, Brook Bhagat, Elisa Carlsen, Tara Stillions Whitehead, and Anne Leigh Parrish.

Learn more at unsolicitedpress.com. Find us on Instagram, X, Facebook, Pinterest, Bsky, Threads, YouTube, and LinkedIn. Unsolicited Press also writes a snarky newsletter on Substack.

www.ingramcontent.com/pod-product-compliance
Lightning Source LLC
Chambersburg PA
CBHW031243120626
46545CB00007B/2629